The New Novello Choral Edition

HEINRICH SCHÜTZ

Christmas Story

Historia der Geburt Jesu Christi (SWV435, 435a)

for soprano, tenor and bass soloists, choir and orchestra

Vocal score
(English/German)

Edited with a new translation by Neil Jenkins

Order No: NOV 072525

NOVELLO PUBLISHING LIMITED

It is requested that on all concert notices and programmes acknowledgement is made to 'The New Novello Choral Edition'.
Es wird gebeten, auf sämtlichen Konzertankfündigungen und Programmen 'The New Novello Choral Edition' als Quelle zu erwähnen.
Il est exigé que toutes notices et programmes de concerts, comportent des remerciements à 'The New Novello Choral Edition'.

Orchestral material is available on hire from the Publisher.
Orchestermaterial ist beim Verlag erhältlich.
Les partitions d'orchestre sont en location disponibles chez l'editeur.

Permission to reproduce from the Preface of this Edition must be obtained from the Publisher.
Die Erlaubnis, das Vorwort dieser Ausgabe oder Teile desselben zu reproduzieren, muß beim Verlag eingeholt werden.
Le droit de reproduction de ce document à partir de la préface doit être obtenu de l'éditeur.

Cover illustration: facsimile of the first page of the part of the Evangelist in the Heinrich Schütz's *Christmas Story* (*Historia der Geburt Jesu Christi*, 1660). Reproduced with the permission of the Library of the University of Uppsala, Sweden.

© 2000 Novello & Company Limited

Published in Great Britain by Novello Publishing Limited
Head office: 14-15 Berners Street, London, W1T 3LJ
Tel +44 (0)20 7612 7400   Fax +44 (0)20 7612 7546

Sales and Hire: Music Sales Distribution Centre
Newmarket Road, Bury St Edmunds, Suffolk, IP33 3YB
Tel +44 (0)1284 702600   Fax +44 (0)1284 768301

Web: www.musicsales.com   e-mail: music@musicsales.co.uk

All rights reserved   Printed in Great Britain

Music setting by Stave Origination

German translation of Preface by Dorothée Goebel

CONTENTS

PREFACE

INTRODUCTION

Schütz composed *The Christmas Story* towards the end of a long and full life. It was probably first performed on Christmas Day 1660 at the Elector of Saxony's Court Chapel in Dresden, since the court diaries for that year refer to the Christmas music in 1660 as 'the Birth of Christ in recitative style'[1]. In his preface to the Evangelist's part (1664), Schütz claimed that the *Christmas Story* introduced the Italian secco recitative to northern Germany, and so the reference is most likely to be to this work, where the composer states:

'...the author will gladly let understanding musicians judge how far he succeeded or failed in this new style, never, so far as he knows, presented in Germany before: - a stilo recitativo for the Evangelist, new both as regards melody and time.'

In this 1664 publication the remaining sections of the work, the eight Intermedia and opening and closing choruses, were advertised as being available for hire.

Not all the music of the *Christmas Story* has survived. The urtext for what has is an amalgam of several sources; Schütz had not intended to publish the work in its entirety. He believed that it was unlikely to achieve its proper effect unless the resources and expertise of 'well established princely chapels' were available for its performance. Schütz also hoped to profit financially profit by only making these movements available through his appointed intermediaries Sebastien Knüpfer, kantor in Leipzig, and Alexander Hering, organist of the Kreuzkirche in Dresden.

Schütz did suggest an alternative to hiring his material by allowing performers the option of interpolating other motets of their choice:

'...moreover, he leaves those who may wish to use his music for the Evangelist to adapt these ten concerted pieces (of which the texts are included in these printed copies) to their pleasure and the musical forces at their disposal: or even to have them composed by someone else.'

The stages by which the *Christmas Story* was gradually pieced together over the last century are outlined below:

1885　The publication of the 1664 edition of the Evangelist's role ('der Chor des Evangelisten') in the first volume of *H. Schütz: Sämtliche Werke* edited by Philipp Spitta. This 1664 edition, printed in Dresden by Wolgang Seyffert, comprises three printed part books, containing the voice part, the organ part and the continuo string bass part ('für die Bass-Geige oder violon').

1908　The discovery, by Arnold Schering, at Uppsala (in the Düben collection) of manuscript part books of a nearly complete version dating from 1660 when the work was first performed. It contains a more primitive version of the Evangelist's part, together with all the Intermedia and the final chorus.

1909　Publication of the material found in Uppsala, edited by Schering, as volume seventeen of *H. Schütz: Sämtliche Werke*. Both versions of the Evangelist's part are shown.

1933　The discovery, by Max Schneider, in the Library of the Berlin Singakademie, of a further incomplete version in part books, now known as the Berliner Fassung[2]. This set of parts is particularly valuable because it shows some of the revisions and improvements which Schütz made to his work in 1671, the year before his death. It also supplies the first fifteen bars of the missing second trombone part to Intermedium 5.

Since the work has been assembled it has formed the basis of the following editions; Fritz Stein (1935), Arthur Mendel (1949), Friedrich Schöneich (1955) and, most recently, the edition edited by Günter Graulich for the Stuttgarter Schütz-Ausgabe (1998).

The Uppsala parts are full inconsistencies and mistakes: it has been suggested that they were compiled for a particular performance[3], and therefore do not necessarily represent Schütz's actual part-writing. There are six instrumental lines plus continuo in the closing chorus, while the original caption indicates 'cum 4 instruments', and the list published in the original Evangelist's part mentions '5 Instrumental Stimmen'. Mendel[4] suggests that these extant parts reveal an anonymous Capellmeister taking up Schütz's invitation to suit the orchestra to the occasion, and making rather a hash of the two trombone parts in the process.

The only surviving music for the opening chorus is the figured bass part (that also shows in which bar the voices enter). In this edition I have been fortunate to be able to include the reconstruction made by Andrew Parrott[5]. Unlike other reconstructions of this portion of the work, Parrott's is more economically scored for two violins, one viola and bass instruments (including one bassoon), making it more consistent with the Uppsala parts. In the present edition, I prefer the 1664 version of the Evangelist's part since it is more melodically interesting, and rhythmically more fluent, as well as containing Schütz's revised continuo interludes. I have reconstructed the conclusion of the second trombone part in Intermedium 5.

EDITORIAL PROCEDURE

All editorial markings are shown in square brackets. The existing parts of the concerted numbers contain very few tempo indications. The terms 'Presto' and 'Adagio', occurring in the three Intermedia for the Angel (1, 7 and 8), must surely imply something rather different from their current meaning. The editor suggests that the performer should infer 'più mosso' from the term 'Presto', and 'meno mosso' from the term 'Adagio'.

The English text has been placed on top of the original German, and only minor modifications have been made to the original underlay of the syllables. I have endeavoured to retain as much as possible of the Authorised Text of the Gospels of St. Matthew and St. Luke.

I have included some ornamentation for the Evangelist on cue-sized staves above the vocal line at major cadences. Performers should feel free to use this or other stylistically appropriate decorations of their own.

KEY

In addition to editing the *Christmas Story*, Mendel spent much of his time researching and writing about the hotly debated topic of pitch in the sixteenth and seventeenth centuries[6]. Particularly relevant to this present edition is a series of articles[7] where he established – by making particular reference to Praetorius' *Syntagma Musicum* (1618) – that pitch in Germany was a fluid matter, that depending on the idiosyncracies of instrument makers[8]. In doing so, Mendel anticipated Robert Donington's asserts that 'there was no prevailing pitch in Baroque music'[9].

I have chosen to follow the precedent set by Arthur Mendel's edition by transposing the work up a tone[10]. The benefits are that the resultant vocal tessituras are more practical. In Intermedium 5, the low Ds for the basses in bar 20 now become a slightly more manageable E. In the original key, the Intermedia 3 (for three altos) and 4 (for three tenors) in practice call for two altos and one tenor, and two tenors and one baritone respectively to sound comfortable at that pitch. In the higher key I feel confident that there will be an alto in Intermedium 3 with a good low G; whilst Intermedium 4 will require the lowest tenor to go down to a manageable low D. The soprano soloist (the Angel) will need a high A rather than a G.

It is worth noting that Schütz himself leaves the door open for such a transposition by saying, in the preface to his *Becker Psalms* (1661 edition), that 'such transpositions are not only very necessary (especially in those written with high clefs) but also will be found more convenient for singers' voices and be more pleasing on the ear'.

CONTINUO REALISATION

Although in the sources the continuo line is given entirely in long notes, there is evidence that the continuo players of the day did not create a seamless stream of sound, but abbreviated some chords. By the time of Bach's *St Matthew Passion* (1729 and 1736), we find the note values of the autograph score differing from that of the parts; possibly suggesting a convention existed for indicating chord changes by filling the bars

with minims and semibreves, and tying them over until the next change of chord. In practice, the players would be more flexible about playing long or short chords.

There are certain cadences in the work where there is scope for a more elaborate realisation. Schütz himself observed, in the characteristically detailed preface to his *Resurrection Story* (*Historia der Auferstehung Jesu Christi*, 1623) swv50, that occasional 'leuffe oder passaggi' (runs or passage-work) were an essential ingredient of the keyboard accompaniment to the style of recitative he employed. I have filled out the right hand of such passages, but they are by no means any more definitive than the rest of the continuo realisation. This retains the original notation, but also indicates in cue sized notes where shorter chords may be used.

INSTRUMENTATION

The *Christmas Story* calls for two *violettas*, two *violins*, one *viola*, one cello or *viola da gamba*, two flutes or *recorders*, one *bassoon*, two clarini (trumpets) or *cornetts*, two high trombones or *sackbuts* and *organ*. An original instrument performance would call for all of the instruments in italics[11]. All of these parts have been newly engraved and are available on hire from the publisher.

A further benefit of the upward transposition of the present edition is that the music for the two violetti can be played by two violins, since the part is now within their compass (the music for the violetti is shown in the violin parts of this edition). There has been much discussion about Schütz's intentions in writing for the violetta. Praetorius, Schütz's older contemporary, uses the word in 1619 to imply either violin or descant viol. But in *Organographia* he equates it with Klein Lyra: 'The little lyra is like the viola di bracio: hence it is also called the lyra di bracio'. By the end of the century the term certainly meant a lower pitched instrument playing a middle part, such as a viola or small viola da gamba. In his recording, Parrott uses tenor viols, explaining in the programme note that viols have a frequent association with celestial music in the Baroque period. As a practicality, however, many performers will doubtless be happy to employ the two violins, required elsewhere in this work, muted, when the appropriate viols (whether tenor or treble) are hard to come by.

To the list of instruments needed for a performance of the *Christmas Story* could be added some optional continuo instruments: violone and theorbo are mentioned in the 1664 edition and in the Uppsala parts as alternative or additional components to the continuo section. A violone or double bass could be of assistance on the bass line of the opening and closing movements, as well as in Intermedia 4 and 5 (and 3a if played). A theorbo, though not essential, could be used in performances where tenor or treble viols have been chosen for Intermedia 1, 7 and 8, since the Uppsala manuscript of Intermedium 1 includes a figured bass marked 'theorba' in addition to the ones for organ. So, it is possible to conjecture that one instrument accompanied the quiet rocking motif in 3/2 rhythm, and the other accompanied the faster 4/4 section. By inference, this could also be applied to Intermedia 7 and 8.

Following Schütz's suggestion in his preface, that the Intermedia should suit the needs of the performers, I have taken the opportunity of introducing a further concerted movement (Intermedium 3a, No.8a), in order to give the sopranos a moment of their own. Not wishing to introduce a biblical text, I have chosen Schütz's four-part 'Alleluia' from the *Kleine Geistliche Konzerte* swv328 (originally for two sopranos and two tenors). It is introduced into the narrative at the conclusion of the nativity sequence and prior to the Presentation of the Temple. It may, however, be easily omitted by passing from the last bar of No.8 to the first bar of No.8b.

ACKNOWLEDGEMENTS

I would like to thank the University of Uppsala for providing microfilm of the extant material, and the choirs that tried out this edition, helping me to judge the translation's effectiveness and assisting me in eliminating any errors from the scores and parts. They include the Brighton Chamber Choir and the Summer Music choir. Thanks are also due to Hywel Davies for his help in seeing the *Christmas Story* through to publication.

Neil Jenkins
Hove, July 2000

NOTES

1   Joshua Ritkin, 'Schütz' article in *New Grove Dictionary of Music and Musicians* ed. Stanley Sadie, 1980

2   'Zum Weihnachtsoratorium von Heinrich Schütz', *Theodor Kroyer: Festschrift zum sechzigsten Geburtstage* (Regensburg, 1933)

3   Arthur Mendel, preface to *Christmas Story* (New York, 1949)

4   ibid.

5   Recorded by Taverner Consort Choir and Players, conducted by Andrew Parrott (VM5 61353-2)

6   See Mendel *Studies in the History of Musical Pitch* (Amsterdam, 1968); *Pitch in Western Music since 1500* (Acta Musicologica, 1978); 'On the pitch in Bach's time' (*MQ*, xli, 1955). The subject is also covered in the article 'Pitch' by Rhodes and Thomas (*New Grove Dictionary of Music and Musicians* ed. Stanley Sadie, 1980)

7   Arthur Mendel, 'Pitch in the 16th and early 17th centuries', *MQ*, xxxiv, 1948

8   Praetorius noted that organs, especially at Halberstadt and Nordhausen, could be one tone or a tone and a half higher than expected.

9   'The choice of instruments in baroque music', *Early Music*, I/3, 1973.

10 Fritz Stein also came to the same conclusion in the preface to his edition that 'the low notation of the vocal parts allows us to assume that the choral pitch of the seventeenth century was considerably higher than it is in our day, and therefore it appears to be historically justifiable to transpose the whole work up by one tone', but did not actually make the transposition. Other commentators have made this suggestion, see Hans Joachim Moser *Heinrich Schütz his life and work* (Saint Louis, 1959) and Kurt Pahlen *The World of Oratorio* (Aldershot, 1990).

11 It should be noted that Claus Hoffmann argues in 'Die konzertierenden Instrumente in 4. Intermedium' (*Musik und Kirche*, 40, 1970) that the violin parts in Intermedium 4 may have been originally played on clarino horns.

EINLEITUNG

Schütz komponierte seine *Weihnachtshistorie* gegen Ende seines langen und erfüllten Lebens. Das Werk wurde vermutlich am Weihnachtstag 1660 in der Hofkapelle des Kurfürsten von Sachsen uraufgeführt. In den Hoftagebüchern wird für jenes Jahr als weihnachtliche Musik festgehalten: 'die Geburt Christi in stilo recitativo'[1]. In seinem Vorwort zu der 1664 im Druck erschienenen Partie des Evangelisten nahm Schütz für sein Werk in Anspruch, daß er in der *Weihnachtshistorie* das italienische Secco-Rezitativ nach Norddeutschland eingeführt habe. Aus diesem Grund liegt die Vermutung nahe, daß es sich bei dem 1660 musizierten Werk um seine Weihnachtshistorie gehandelt habe, über die Schütz weiter schreibt:

> Und läßet Herr Autor im übrigen, wie weit dieser des Evangelistens im Stylo Recitativo neue, und bißhero in Teutschland seines Wissens, in Druck noch nie herfür gekommene Aufsatz [Satzart], beides mit der über die Worte von Ihm geführten Modulation und Mensur, Ihm gelungen oder mißlungen sei, verständige Musicos gerne davon urtheilen.

In dieser Publikation aus dem Jahr 1664 wurden die übrigen Abschnitte des Werkes, die acht Intermedien, und die beiden sie umrahmenden Chorsätze, Introduktion und Beschluß, leihweise angeboten. Die *Weihnachtshistorie* ist nicht komplett erhalten. Der 'Urtext' ist ein Konglomerat aus verschiedenen Quellen. Schütz hatte nicht beabsichtigt, sein Werk zur Gänze zum Druck zu geben. 'Gebührenden Effekt' könne das Werk nur erzielen, wenn es mit den Ressourcen und Erfahrungen 'fürstlicher wohlbestälter Capellen' musiziert werde. Schütz erhoffte sich Einnahmen, indem er diese Teile nur durch eigens ausgesuchte Mittler, nämlich Sebastian Knüpfer, Kantor in Leipzig, und Alexander Hering, Organist der Kreuzkirche in Dresden zugänglich machte.

Neben dem Beziehen des des Notenmaterials erlaubte Schütz noch eine weitere Möglichkeit: Interpreten könnten auch Motetten eigener Wahl in das Werk einfügen, falls sie nicht seine Werke musizieren wollten:

> Massen denn auch hierüber noch, Er denenjenigen, welche dieses seines Evangelistens, sich zu gebrauchen Luft haben möchten, es frey stellen thut, solche Zehen Concerten (: derer Texte auff diesen Abdrücken, auch mit zu befinden sind :) auff die ihnen beliebende Manier und verhandenes Corpus Musicum, gar auffs neue anders selbst aufzusetzen, oder durch andere componiren zu lassen.

Während des letzten Jahrhunderts wurden die einzelnen Elemente der *Weihnachtshistorie* allmählich zusammengeführt. Im folgenden wird dieser Prozeß kurz skizziert:

1885 Veröffentlichung der gedruckten Evangelistenpartie aus dem Jahr 1664 ("der Chor des Evangelisten") im ersten Band der von Philipp Spitta herausgegebenen Gesamtausgabe der Werke von Heinrich Schütz. Diese 1664 von Wolfgang Seyffert in Dresden gedruckte Fassung besteht aus drei gedruckten Stimmbüchern, nämlich der Gesangsstimme, der Orgelstimme und der Continuo-Stimme für ein Streichinstrument ('für die Bass-Geige oder violon').

1908 Arnold Schering entdeckte in der Düben-Sammlung in Uppsala eine fast vollständige Fassung aus dem Jahr der ersten Aufführung, 1660, in handschriftlichen Stimmbüchern. Dieses Quellenmaterial enthält eine schlichtere Fassung der Evangelistenpartie, sämtliche Intermedien und den abschließenden Schlußchor.

1909 Das in Uppsala aufgefundene Material wurde von Schering als Band 17 der Schütz-Gesamtausgabe publiziert. In dieser Veröffentlichung wurden beide Fassungen der Evangelistenpartie mitgeteilt.

1933 Max Schneider entdeckte in der Bibliothek der Berliner Singakademie eine weitere unvollständige Fassung in Stimmbüchern, heute als sogenannte 'Berliner Fassung'[2] bezeichnet. Diese Stimmbücher sind von besonderem Wert, da aus ihnen einige der Revisionen und Verbesserungen ersichtlich werden, die Schütz in seinem Werk 1671 im Jahr vor seinem Tod vornahm. Diese Fassung enthält für das Intermedium 5 außerdem die ersten fünfzehn Takte der fehlenden Partie der zweiten Posaune.

Diese Quellen wurden zur Grundlage für die folgenden Ausgaben: Fritz Stein (1935), Arthur Mendel (1949), Friedrich Schöneich (1955) und als letztes schließlich die von Günter Graulich für die Stuttgarter Schütz-Ausgabe (1998) edierte Fassung.

Die Stimmen aus Uppsala weisen zahlreiche Unstimmigkeiten auf und sind voller Fehler. In der Forschung wurde die These vertreten, daß sie für eine einzelne Aufführung bestimmt waren und deshalb nicht notwendigerweise Schütz endgültige Fassung der Stimmen darstellten[3]. Der abschließende Chorsatz ist in der Quelle in Uppsala mit sechs Instrumentalstimmen und Continuo besetzt, während die ursprüngliche Überschrift lautet 'mit 4 Instrumenten'. Die Druckfassung der Evangelistenpartie dagegen verzeichnet '5 Instrumental Stimmen'. Mendel[4] stellt die Vermutung auf, daß es sich bei den in Uppsala überlieferten Stimmen um das Werk eines anonymen Kapellmeisters handle, der Schütz Vorschlag folgt, das Orchester je nach den Gegenbenheiten einzurichten und dabei die beiden Posaunenstimmen in erheblichem Maße korrumpierte.

Vom Eingangschor ist nur der bezifferte Baß erhalten (in dieser Stimme sind die verschiedenen Stimm-Einsätze angegeben). In der vorliegenden Ausgabe konnte ich freundlicherweise auf die von Andrew Parrott vorgelegte Rekonstruktion dieses Satzes zurückgreifen[5]. Parrott instrumentiert diesen Teil des Werkes im Gegensatz zu anderen Musikern recht sparsam. Er besetzt mit zwei Violinen, einer Viola und Instrumenten der Baß-Gruppe (darunter ein Fagott), so daß seine Rekonstruktion besser mit den in Uppsala überlieferten Stimmbüchern harmoniert.

In der vorliegenden Ausgabe gebe ich der Evangelistenpartie aus der Fassung von 1664 gegenüber der früheren Fassung den Vorzug, da sie melodisch interessanter ist und rhythmisch einen gleichmässigeren Fluß aufweist. Außerdem enthält diese Fassung Schütz revidierten Continuo-Zwischenspiele. Die fehlenden Teile der zweiten Posaunenstimme aus Intermedium 5 habe ich ergänzt.

ZUR EDITION

Alle Zusätze des Herausgebers sind durch eckige Klammern gekennzeichnet. Die überlieferten Stimmen der Konzerte (Intermedien) enthalten nur äußerst wenige Tempovorschriften. Die Tempobezeichnungen 'Presto' und 'Adagio' aus den drei Intermedien mit dem Engel (1, 7, und 8) sind sicher anders als ihrer heutigen Bedeutung gesetzt. Der Herausgeber schlägt dem Interpreten vor, das 'Presto' als 'Più mosso' und das 'Adagio' als 'Meno mosso' zu verstehen.

Der englische Text wurde über den originalen deutschen Text gelegt. Dabei wurde von der ursprünglichen syllabischen Anordnung nur geringfügig abgewichen. Ich habe mich darum bemüht, die gültige Textfassung der Evangelien nach Matthäus und Lukas so weit als möglich beizubehalten.

Bei wichtigen kadenzierenden Abschnitten habe ich einige Verzierungsvorschläge für den Evangelisten auf einem kleiner gestochenen System oberhalb der Gesangsstimme angegeben. Die Interpreten sollten diese oder andere stilistisch passende eigene Verzierungen verwenden.

ZUR TONART

Neben seiner Edition der *Weihnachtshistorie* beschäftigte Mendel sich intensiv forschend und publizierend mit der vielfach diskutierten Frage nach dem Stimmton im 16. und 17. Jahrhundert[6]. Von besonderer Bedeutung für die vorliegende Ausgabe sind einige Artikel[7], in denen er vor allem im Rückgriff auf Praetorius Syntagma Musicum (1618) feststellte, daß es in Deutschland keinen verbindlichen Stimmton gab. Der Stimmton beruhte vielmehr auf den charakteristischen Vorlieben der Instrumentenbauer[8]. Mendel nahm hierin Robert Doningtons Behauptungen vorweg, 'daß es in der Musik des Barock keinen einheitlichen Stimmton gegeben habe'[9].

Ich bin in meiner Ausgabe dem Beispiel von Arthur Mendel gefolgt, indem ich das Werk um einen Ganzton nach oben transponiert habe[10]. Die sich hieraus ergebenden Stimmumfänge sind für die Praxis günstiger. Aus dem D in den Bässen in Takt 20 wird so ein etwas leichter erreichbares E. Wenn man Intermedium 3 (für drei Alt-Stimmen) und 4 (für drei Tenöre) in der originalen Fassung musiziert, wird man zur Erzielung eines akzeptablen Klanges in dieser Lage mit zwei Altistinnen und einem Tenor, beziehungsweise mit zwei Tenören und einem Bariton besetzen müssen. Ich bin mir sicher, daß eine Altistin im dritten Intermedium nach der Transposition ein gutes G singen kann; im vierten Intermedium muß der tiefste Tenor nach der Transposition bis zu einem erreichbaren D nach unten gehen. Nach der Transposition erreicht der Solo-Sopran (der Engel) A anstelle von G.

An dieser Stelle bleibt festzuhalten, daß Schütz selber die Möglichkeit einer Transposition offenhält. Er schreibt im Vorwort zu seinem *Becker-Psalter* (Ausgabe von 1661): 'Sintemahl solche Transpositionem bey Gebrauch dieses Wereleins offtermals nicht alleine hochnöthig sondern auch der Cantorum Stimmen bequem und dem Gehör desto angenehm fallen.'

ZUR CONTINUO-AUSSETZUNG

Auch wenn die Continuo-Stimme in den Quellen ausschließlich in langen Notenwerten notiert ist, musizierten die Continuo-Spieler jener Tage nicht eine ununterbrochene Folge von Tönen, sondern verkürzten einige Akkorde. Bei Bachs *Matthäus-Passion* (1729 und 1736) sehen wir, daß die Notenwerte in der autographen Partitur und in den Stimmen sich voneinander unterscheiden. Möglicherweise ist das ein Hinweis auf eine Notationsform, mit der auf Akkordwechsel hingewiesen wurde: die Takte wurden mit Halben und Ganzen ausgefüllt, die bis zum darauffolgenden Akkordwechsel übergebunden wurden. Heutige Spieler sollten bei sich bei der Verwendung länger ausgehaltener oder kürzerer Akkorde flexibel zeigen.

Es gibt einige Kadenzen im Werk, bei denen sich eine stärker ausgearbeitete Realisierung anbietet. Schütz formulierte in seiner auf charakteristische Weise ausführlichen Einleitung zu seiner *Historia der Auferstehung Jesu Christi* aus dem Jahr 1623 (swv50), daß gelegentliche 'leuffe oder passaggi' bei seinen Rezitativen ein wesentliches Gestaltungselement auf dem begleitenden Tasteninstrument bedeuteten. Solche Realisationen habe ich für die rechte Hand notiert; diese beanspruchen gegenüber der sonstigen Continuo-Aussetzung aber keineswegs größere Verbindlichkeit. Die originalen Notenwerte wurden in der Aussetzung beibehalten, Noten im Kleinstich weisen auf Akkorde hin, die man verkürzer könnte.

ZUR INSTRUMENTIERUNG

Die *Weihnachtshistorie* ist geschrieben für zwei *Violettas*, zwei *Violinen*, eine *Bratsche*, ein *Violoncello* oder *Viola da gamba*, zwei *Flöten* oder *Blockflöten*, ein *Fagott*, zwei *Clarini* (Trompeten) oder *Zinken*, zwei hohe *Posaunen* und *Orgel*. Bei einer Ausführung mit Originalinstrumenten müßte man die in Kursiva gesetzten Instrumenten besetzen[11]. Alle Stimmen wurden neu gestochen und sind leihweise beim Verlag erhältlich.

Ein weiterer Vorteil der in unserer Ausgabe vorgenommenen Transposition um einen Ganzton nach oben liegt darin, daß die Stimmen der beiden Violetti nun aufgrund des veränderten Tonumfangs auf der Violine auszuführen sind, (die Stimmen der Violetti sind in den Violinstimmen unserer Edition enthalten). Schütz Einsatz der Violetti ist vielfach diskutiert worden. Praetorius, der ältere Zeitgenosse von Schütz, verwendet das Wort 1619 sowohl für die Violine wie für die Diskant-Gambe. In seiner *Organographia* setzt er dagegen die Violetta mit der kleinen Lyra gleich: 'Die kleine Lyra ist der Tenor Violen de bracio gleich: Daher sie auch Lyra de bracio gennant wird'. Zum Ende des Jahrhunderts hin verstand man unter der Violetta zweifellos ein Instrument mittlerer Stimmlage zur Ausführung von Mittelstimmen, wie eine Bratsche oder eine kleine Viola da gambe. Parrott verwendet bei seiner Einspielung Tenorgamben und weist im Beitext darauf hin, daß man zur Barockzeit Gamben häufig mit himmlischer Musik assoziierte. Aus rein praktischen Gründen wird man sich bei vielen Aufführungen aber gerne der zwei Violinen bedienen, die an anderer Stelle im Stück eingesetzt werden, wenn Gamben (seien es nun Tenor- oder Soprangamben) nicht greifbar sind. Die Violinen sollten in diesem Fall mit Dämpfer gespielt werden.

Die Liste der für eine Aufführung der *Weihnachtshistorie* notwendigen Instrumente ließe sich noch um einiges erweitern: Violone und Theorbe werden in der Ausgabe 1664 und in den Stimmen aus Uppsala als Alternative oder Ergänzung beim Continuo erwähnt. Ein Violone oder Kontrabaß wäre zur Ausführung der Baß-Stimme bei Eingangs- wie Schlußsatz denkbar, auch in den Intermedien 4 und 5 (sowie 3a, wenn dieser Teil gespielt wird). Auch wenn eine Theorbe nicht unabdingbar ist, könnte sie doch bei Aufführungen eingesetzt werden, in denen Tenor- oder Soprangamben für die Intermedien 1, 7 und 8 Verwendung finden. Schließlich enthält das Manuskript von Intermedium 1 in Uppsala neben der Orgelstimme eine bezifferte und mit 'Theorba' bezeichete weitere Baß-Stimme Daraus läßt sich folgern, daß ein Instrument das ruhige, schaukelnde Motiv im 3/2-Rhythmus begleitete, das andere die schnelleren Abschnitte im 4/4-Takt. Eine ähnliche Instrumentation ließe sich daraus auch für die Intermedien 7 und 8 ableiten.

In Übereinstimmung mit dem Vorschlag von Schütz in dessen Vorwort die Intermedien den Möglichkeiten der Interpreten anzupassen habe ich mir erlaubt, einen weiteren Satz einzufügen (das Intermedium 3a, Nr. 8a), um den Sopranen einen eigenen Wirkungsbereich zu geben. Da ich keinen biblischen Text ergänzen wollte, habe ich Schütz vierstimmiges 'Alleluia' swv328 aus den *Kleinen Geistlichen Konzerten II* ausgewählt (im Original für zwei Soprane und zwei Tenöre gesetzt). Es wird in die Satzfolge am Ende des Weihnachtsgeschehens und vor der Darstellung im Tempel eingeschoben. Dieses Musikstück kann man jedoch leicht auslassen, indem man vom letzten Takt der Nr. 8 gleich zum ersten Takt von Nr. 8b springt.

DANKSAGUNGEN

Der Universität von Uppsala möchte ich für die Übermittlung von Mikrofilmen des dort liegenden Materials danken. Mein Dank gebührt auch den Chören, darunter dem Brighton chamber choir und dem Summer Music choir, die mit mir die vorliegende Edition durchgesungen haben. Auf diese Weise konnte ich die Sangbarkeit der Übersetzung prüfen und Fehler in Partituren und Stimmen eliminieren. Danken möchte ich auch Hywel Davies für seine Hilfe bei der Drucklegung der *Weihnachtshistorie*.

Neil Jenkins
Hove
Juli 2000

1   Joshua Rifkin, Artikel 'Heinrich Schütz' in *New Grive Dictionary of Music and Musicians*, hrsg. von Stanley Sadie, 1980.
2   "Zum Weihnachtsoratorium von Heinrich Schütz", in: *Theodor Kroyer: Festschrift zum sechzigsten Geburtstage*, Regensburg 1933.
3   Arthur Mendel, Vorwort zu seiner Ausgabe von Heinrich Schütz *Weihnachtshistorie*, New York 1949.
4   A.a.O.
5   Eine Aufnahme dieser Fassung mit dem Taverner Consort Choir and Players unter der Leitung von Andrew Parrott ist bei VM5 61353.2 eingespielt.
6   Siehe hierzu Mendel, *Studies in the History of Musical Pitch*, Amsterdam 1968; "Pitch in Western Music since 1500", in: *Acta Musicologica* 1978; "On the pitch in Bach's time", in: *Musical Quarterly* XLI, 1955. Vgl. hierzu auch den Artikel "Pitch" von Rhodes und Thomas in *New Grove Dictionary of Music and Musicians*, hrsg. von Stanley Sadie, 1980.
7   Arthur Mendel, "Pitch in the 16th and early 17th centuries", in: *Musical Quarterly* XXXIV, 1948.
8   Praetorius schreibt, daß die Stimmung der Orgeln, vor allem in Halberstadt und Nordhausen, zwischen einem Ganzton oder sogar drei Halbtöne höher als erwartet liegen konnte.
9   "The choice of instruments in baroque music", in: *Early Music* I/3, 1973.
10 Fritz Stein kam im Vorwort seiner Ausgabe zu demselben Schluß, ohne eine solche Transposition dann allerdings in der Edition durchzuführen. Er schreibt: "die tiefe Lage der Vokalpartien erlaubt die Annahme, daß der Stimmton der Chöre im 17. Jahrhundert bedeutend höher war als heute. Deshalb erscheint es historisch vertretbar, das ganze Werk um einen Ton nach oben zu transponieren." Auch andere Autoren haben diesen Vorschlag gemacht, vgl. Hans Joachim Moser, *Heinrich Schütz. Sein Leben und Werk*, zweite Auflage Kassel 1954, und Kurt Pahlen, *Oratorien der Welt*, Zürich 1985.
11 Claus Hoffmann vertritt in seinem Artikel "Die konzertierenden Instrumente im 4. Intermedium" in: *Musik und Kirche* 40, 1970 die Auffassung, daß die Violinstimmen im vierten Intermedium ursprünglich vielleicht auf Clarin-Hörnern gespielt wurden.

THE CHRISTMAS STORY
HISTORIA DER GEBURT JESU CHRISTI

swv435, 435a

HEINRICH SCHÜTZ
edited and translated by Neil Jenkins

No. 1

INTRODUCTION or PROLOGUE *
to the Birth of our Lord Jesus Christ
INTRODUCTION oder EINGANG zu der Geburt unsers Herren Jesu Christ

Chorus SATB

* see Preface

* Uppsala MS has

No. 2

[Recitative]
Evangelist

Luke ii, 1-10

* A minim might be preferable here.

8

came the time that she should be de - liv - - - ered, and she brought
kam die zeit, daß sie ge - bä - ren soll - - te, und sie ge-

7   6

forth her_ first -born son, and wrap -ped_ Him in_ swad -dling clothes, and laid the ba - by
-bar ih -ren er - sten Sohn und wik - kelt_ ihn in_ Win - - deln und leg - te ihn in

5   6   7   6

in a man - ger, for there was at that time no room for them in the
ei - ne Krip - -pen, denn sie hat -ten sonst kei -nen Raum in der Her - ber-

[7] [6] # ♭   3 4 4 3

inn.   Now   in   that same
- ge.   *Und   es   wa - ren*

[p]

4 3   ♭   [p]

coun - try, a - bi -ding in the_ fields there were some shep -herds, who kept a care -ful watch o'er their
Hir - ten in der -sel -bi -gen Ge -gend auf dem Fel - de, die hü -te -ten des Nachts ih -re

♭   ♭   ♭

* b.46, beats 1 and 2 omitted in the Berlin Fassung

No. 3   INTERMEDIUM 1
The Angel to the Shepherds in the fields wherein is introduced, from time to time,
the rocking of the Christchild's cradle
*Der Engel zu den Hirten auf dem Felde, worunter bisweilen des
Christkindleins Wiege mit eingeführet wird*
Soprano Solo

Luke ii, 10-12

Sinfonia

10

* The length of this note is left to the discretion of the performer (there are no pauses shown in the instrumental or continuo parts at this point).

* see Preface

† The length of this note is left to the discretion of the performer (there are no pauses shown in the instrumental or continuo parts at this point).

No. 4

[Recitative]
Evangelist

Luke ii, 13

EVANGELIST
[f]

And there sud-den-ly was with the an-gel a mul-ti-tude of the heav'n-ly
Und als-bald__ war da bei dem En-gel die Men-ge der himm-li-schen Herr-

Cont. [f]

host, who were all prai-sing God and__ say - - - ing:
-scha - ren, die lo - be - ten Gott und__ spra - - - chen:

4   #   6   7   6

No. 5

INTERMEDIUM 2
The chorus of Angels
Die Menge der Engel
Chorus SSATTB

Luke ii, 14

Chorus
SOPRANO 1
[f]

Glo - - - ry__ to__ God, glo - - - ry__ to__
Eh - - - re__ sei__ Gott, Eh - - - re__ sei

SOPRANO 2
[f]

Glo - - - ry__ to__ God,
Eh - - - re__ sei__ Gott,

ALTO
[f]

Glo - - -
Eh - - -

TENOR 1

TENOR 2

BASS

Vlns., Bsn. [f]
Cont.

20

* Uppsala MS has ○

24

No. 6

[Recitative]
Evangelist

Luke ii, 15

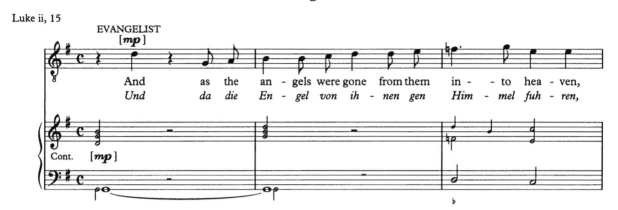

And as the an - gels were gone from them in - - to hea - ven,
Und da die En - gel von ih - nen gen Him - mel fuh - ren,

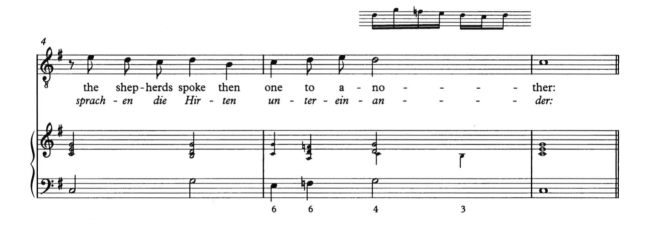

the shep - herds spoke then one to a - no - - - - - ther:
sprach - en die Hir - ten un - ter - ein - an - - - - - der:

No. 7

INTERMEDIUM 3
The Shepherds in the field
Die Hirten auf dem Felde
AAA*

Luke ii, 15

* 3 solo voices (usually from the choir)

* Uppsala part has "vel in Tenore" suggesting that a tenor could sing this part.

No. 8

[Recitative]
Evangelist

Luke ii, 16-20

28

29

* b.17, beats 2 and 3 omitted in the Berlin Fassung
† b.33, beats 1 and 2 omitted in the Berlin Fassung

No. 8a

INTERMEDIUM 3a
Alleluja *
SSSS†

* see Preface   † 4 solo voices (usually from the choir)
** Soprano 3 and 4 may be sung by Tenor 1 and 2 respectively.

No. 8b

[Recitative]
Evangelist

Luke ii, 21
Matthew ii, 1

there came from the East three— Wise Men, go-ing to Je-ru-sa-lem and say — — ing:
da ka-men die Wei-sen aus Mor-gen-lan-de gen Je-ru-sa-lem und spra — — chen:

5 6 # [4] [3]

No. 9

INTERMEDIUM 4
The Wise Men from the East
Die Weisen aus Morgenlande
TTT*

Matthew ii, 2

Sinfonia

Vlns., Bsn.,
Cont. [*f*]

6

5

TENOR 1 [*f*]

Where
Wo

TENOR 2 [*f*]

Where is the new-born King of Is-rael,
Wo ist der neu-ge-bor-ne Kö-nig,

TENOR 3 [*f*]

Where is the new-born King of
Wo ist der neu-ge-bor-ne

9

6 [6 5] 6 6

* 3 solo voices (usually from the choir)

36

6

38

* Uppsala MS has 𝆷

No. 10

[Recitative]
Evangelist

Matthew ii, 3-5

No. 11

INTERMEDIUM 5
The High Priests and the Scribes
Hohepriester und Schriftgelehrte
BBBB*

Matthew ii, 5-6

* 4 solo voices (usually from the choir)
† see Preface for reference to the completion of the 2nd Trombone part.

44

* Uppsala MS has even quavers: ♪. ♪ would be consistent with bb. 40, 49-55

43

-rael, for from thee there shall come forth
sei, denn aus dir soll mir kom- -men

-rael, for from thee there shall come forth_
sei, denn aus dir soll mir kom-men_ a rul- -
der Her-

-rael, for from thee there shall come forth a rul- -
sei, denn aus dir soll mir kom- -men der Her-

-rael, for from thee there shall come forth a rul- -
sei, denn aus dir soll mir kom- -men der Her-

47

a rul - er, and he shall be a migh -ty King,
der Her - zog, der ü - ber mein Volk Is - ra -el,

-er, and he shall be a migh -ty King of
-zog, der ü - ber mein Volk Is - ra -el ein

-er, and he shall be a migh -ty King,
-zog, der ü - ber mein Volk Is - ra -el,

-er, and he shall be a migh-ty King,
-zog, der ü - ber mein Volk Is - ra -el,

* Uppsala MS has ⌐⌐

No. 12

[Recitative]
Evangelist

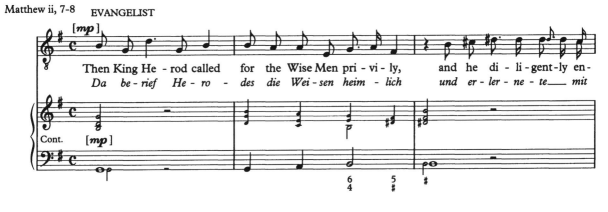

No. 13   INTERMEDIUM 6
King Herod
Herodes
Bass solo

Matthew ii, 8

* Uppsala MS has a definite ♯ here, but no accidentals in the Clarino parts in b.38.

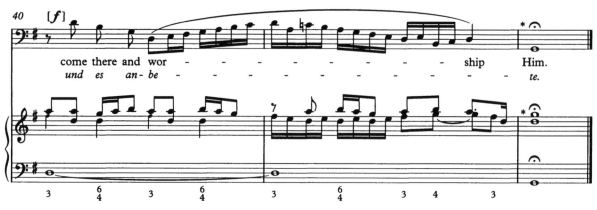

No. 14

[Recitative]

Evangelist

Matthew ii, 9-13

* Uppsala MS has

29
God in a dream, that they should not re-turn a-gain in-to the land of He-rod, they de-
ih-nen im Traum, daß sie sich nicht soll-ten wie-der zu He-ro-des len-ken, und sie

33
-part-ed and took an-oth-er way back to their own land.
zo-gen durch ei-nen an-dern Weg wie-der in ihr Land.

6 4 3

36
[mp]
Af - ter this, when the Wise Men had de-part-ed,
Da sie a - ber hin-weg ge-zo-gen wa-ren,
[mp]
5 6 #

40
Lo! then, there ap-peared the an-gel of the Lord un-to Jo-seph in a dream, and said:
sie-he, da er-schien der En - gel des Her-ren dem Jo-seph im Traum und sprach:
6 5 6 [#]

* b. 35, beats 1 and 2 omitted in the Berlin Fassung

No. 15

INTERMEDIUM 7
The Angel to Joseph
wherein the rocking of the Christchild's cradle is introduced again
Der Engel zu Joseph
Darinnen abermals des Christkindleins Wiege eingeführet wird
Soprano Solo

Matthew ii, 13

* see Preface

* see Preface

No. 16

[Recitative]
Evangelist

Matthew ii. 14-19

* see Preface
† The length of this note is left to the discretion of the performer. **Uppsala MS has ⌐⌐

No. 17

INTERMEDIUM 8
The Angel to Joseph
wherein the rocking of the Christchild's cradle is introduced one more time
Der Engel zu Joseph
Worunter wiederum des Christkindleins Weige eingeführet wird
Soprano Solo

Matthew ii, 20

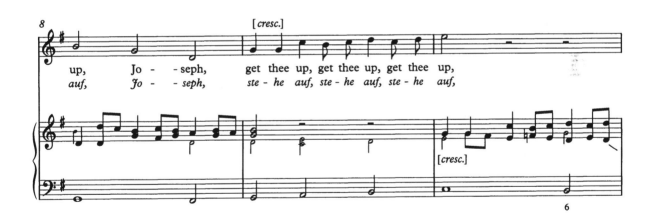

Adagio*

Get thee up, and take the Christ-child and take His mo—ther with—— thee.

Ste - he auf, und nimm das Kind - lein und sei - ne Mut - - ter zu—— dir.

[Tempo I]

Get thee up, get thee up, get thee up, Jo—seph.

Ste - he auf, ste - he auf, ste - he auf, Jo - seph.

Adagio*

Get thee up, and take the Christ-child, and take His mo—ther with thee, and go—— forth, and go—— forth now in-to Is-ra-

Ste - he auf, und nimm das Kind - lein und sei - ne Mut - ter zu dir, und zeuch—— hin, und zeuch—— hin in das Land Is - ra-

* see Preface

* The length of this note is left to the discretion of the performer.

† Uppsala MS has 𝅗𝅥

No. 18

[Recitative]
Evangelist

Matthew ii, 21-23
Luke ii, 40

* in Berlin Fassung:

63

* Uppsala MS has ⌐

No. 19

CONCLUSION
of the Birth of our Lord and Saviour Jesus Christ
BESCHLUSS der Geburt unseres Herrn und Seligmachers Jesu Christi
Chorus SATB

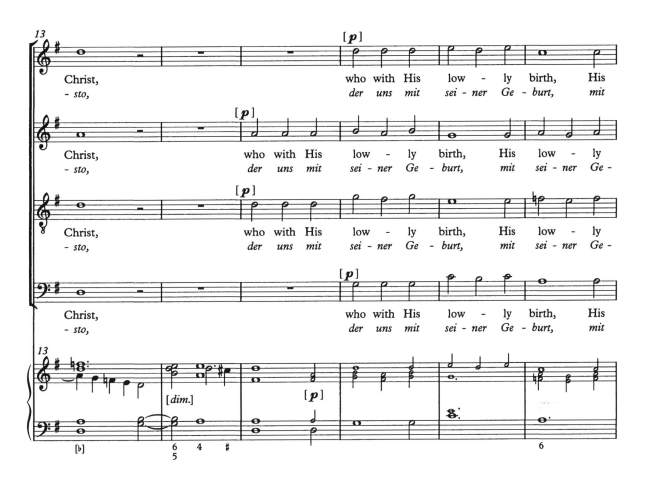

66

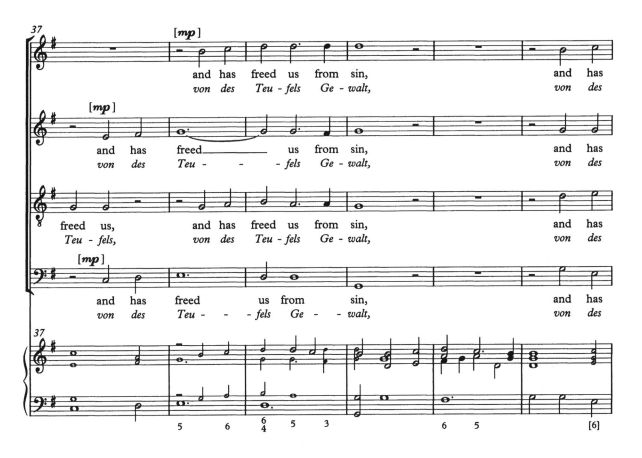

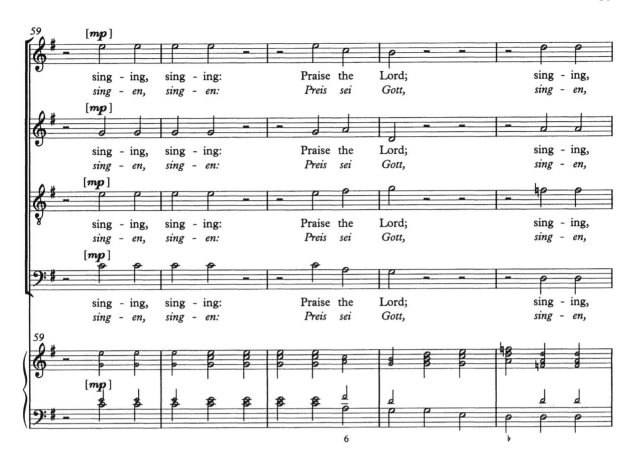

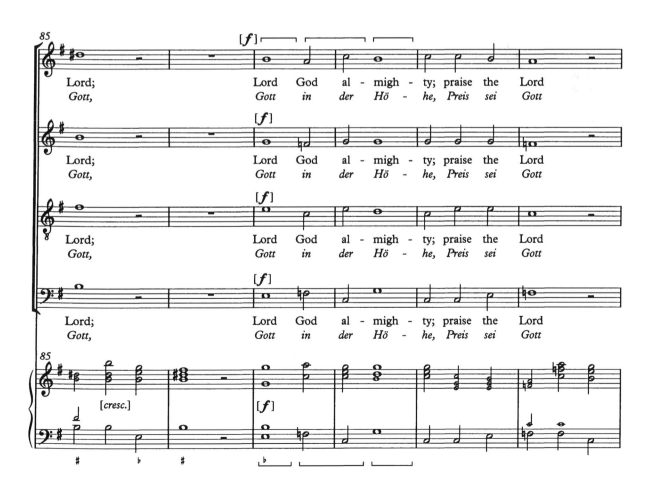

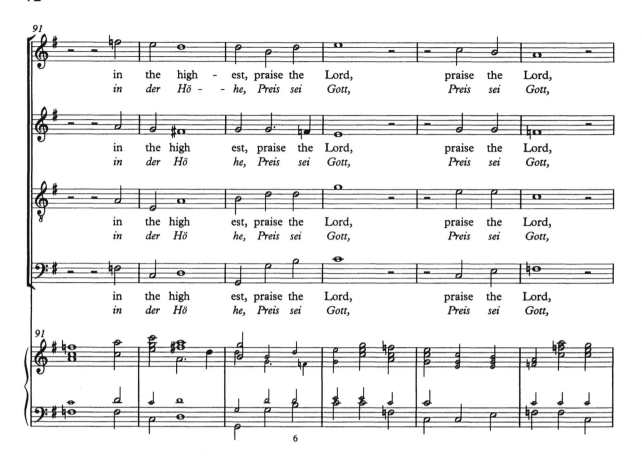

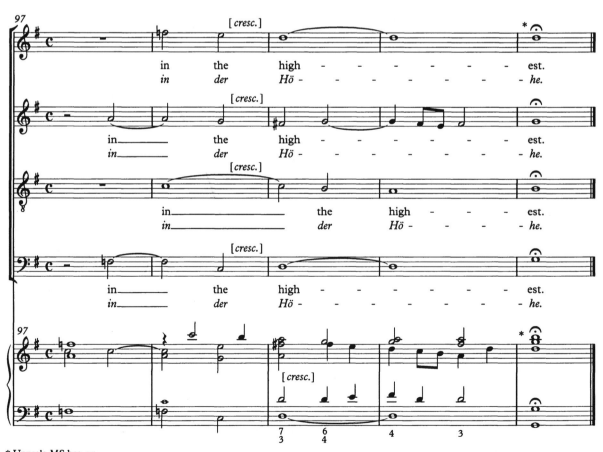

* Uppsala MS has

3456789